QUIET REMNANTS

Bischoff and Swaney

to Jerr and Johnny,
you built us a home with love instead of walls

in loving memory of Harold Swaney

Contents

There are stories lost beneath the floorboards.

There are poems that leak through the cracks in the plaster.

There is a song faintly heard out of the broken windows.

There is a beauty, here, resting in what once was.

Newell, South Dakota

regarding an apparition

There was a moment in time
when bags were packed,
sitting on the front porch
waiting to be taken away.

There was a decision made,
whether it was out of
chaos
or *fright*
or a moment of *calm*,
where someone decided
it was time to move on.

There was a moment that took place
when there was no looking back,
as if the four walls and roof
were ghosts
waiting to get swept up
by the prairie winds.

There was a last drawing of blinds,
like eyes closing before an eternal sleep.

There was a last bath,
a final wash to cleanse one's sins.

There was a last goodnight story,
with one last goodnight kiss.

And one last goodbye,
before the bags on the porch
were picked up
and carried away.

Now here we are,
telling ghost stories
about what we saw
and how we felt
as we contemplate
that moment in time
right before the apparition
was set free.

Tulare, South Dakota

the fading of existence

A seed,
watered with luck,
grows into a towering tree
and lives in oneness
with the dakota soil.

A house,
built by calloused hands,
becomes a shelter
and lives in oneness
next to the towering tree.

Oh, how telling it is
to have two structures
composed of wood
living in unison
and see the tree stand tall
as the residence decays.

We are not meant to last.

Rather,
we are meant
to cherish what we have,
for we flicker
and eventually fade,
just as the stars do.

Murdo, South Dakota

moving on

I peered through a window.

I saw through to the other side
and beyond.

There was such peace
to be found.

Blades of grass gently swaying,
beckoning me
to come dance with them.

An inviting skyline,
with clouds seducing me
to come a little closer.

Between me and this newness
was rotted wood,
a past.

I believe that
even if we let go,
we can always look back and remember.

And one day
when the wood can no longer hold,
it will all come tumbling down.

Here is where
we will become
one with the grass
and one with the clouds.

Carthage, South Dakota

the smell of burning pinewood

*(On June 10th, 1910, a fire struck the business
district of Carthage, South Dakota)*

Locals wandered the sidewalks made of pine
smiling at the passerby,
for there was an abundance of reasons
to give thanks for the summer season.

Conversations rose out of their mouths
like flowers coming into bloom.

The smell of smoke
was the weight that broke
the hopeful rope
that held the town together,
beckoning them out of their front doors.

What they found when they followed their nose
was a multitude of buildings fully engulfed
by a gluttonous flame.

The next morning,
a few blocks from the rubble and ash,
songbirds fluttered their wings.

Their graceful bodies
hovered slightly above the leaves
on bold branches breathing in the morning sun.

Their unwavering toil continued
alongside the fading smoke,
a notion of normalcy
that gave the locals a glimmer of hope
that they'll rebuild their town again.

Colome, South Dakota

forgotten

The prairie wind blows
with an unwavering force,
shaking the ailing walls
of a forgotten prairie home.

Do the floorboards cry out
with their mournful creaks?

Another thunderstorm comes
with a chip on its shoulder,
bringing deafening howls
and streaks of light.

Does the roof shed a tear
with the rainwater that leaks?

Do you ever wonder
if rusted hinges reminisce
about their once vibrant youth,
just as we do?

I think about the wildflowers
that find their refuge next to
a forgotten prairie home and wonder,
do they know something we don't?

I like to believe
that the prairie grass is enlightened,
and its dance with the wind
is meant to tell us something.

I like to believe
that there is life amongst the ruins,
desperate to be noticed.

I'd like to believe
I can slow down just enough
to take it in.

Hecla, South Dakota

perseverance

I took a drive
to clear my mind
on a brisk autumn day.

I stumbled upon
a house still standing
by leafless trees.

There was an obvious,
but slow demise occurring.

Loose siding,
busted windows,
and moss growing from the shingles.

Yet,
here the house was,
still standing.

I thought to myself,
how can I find the
well of steadfastness
this house holds,
and drink from it?

I stood in awe
of the perseverance
spilled by this wise structure
on the midwest prairie.

As I drove back home,
I took with me this house,
and placed it in my chest
so that my heart can lean on it
when the next storm hits.

Spencer, South Dakota

slowing down

There are skeletons that rest gently
on the soil of the dakotas.

Bones made of wood
with hand-driven nails.

Sometimes,
we notice the frailness,
the eerie quiet,
as we take a moment to ponder.

Other times,
we chase the ebb and flow
of our one life
and forget to take the time
to contemplate.

And what do we miss
when we are too busy
to take it all in?

There is a mystery here,
that isn't meant to be answered.

But there is still something to be found,
a *joy*,
a *rebirth*,
that will forever evade us
when we live life with eyes closed.

Pukwana, South Dakota

passersby

The prairie is a place
where passersby ponder
the perfect ruins that pop into sight
as they drive up and down the countryside.

Sometimes I ask myself,
how can something be so haunting,
yet so beautiful?

How can something
be in shambles,
yet perfectly preserve
the essence of its existence?

We see the remnants of an end,
but do you sense,
as I do,
the faint heartbeat?

Do you sense
that there is something
very much alive
inside the remnants?

I believe these ruins
are so much more
than rotting wood
and hand-driven nails.

Hecla, South Dakota

straight lines with crooked sticks

Aren't we all
but a house with no windows?

Aren't we all
hoping to let the light in?

Sometimes,
I wonder why we leave home
to find home,
as what is left behind
turns into remnants
of our innocence.

Quiet Remnants

Now a hollow shell
of rotten wood,
the light still finds a way
to touch the brokenness.

Aren't we all
but a house with no windows?

Exposed to the elements,
but still able to let light in,
and give light to others.

Let your light shine,
like the lantern
that once lit this home
on the loneliness of nights.

Newell, South Dakota

a yearning to know

I sometimes wish
I could have been
a fly on the wall
of abandoned homes
before the homeowners
said their goodbyes.

I would write stories of the happiness
that would spill out of the cracks
in the foundation.

I would write about
the beauty that exists
under the layers and layers of paint.

I would capture the laughter
that would float out the chimney,
just like the smoke from the flames
that existed in the fireplace.

These abandoned homes
are full of stories untold,
the epitome of the beauty
that exists on the midwest prairie.

Chamberlain, South Dakota

glory days

There is an abode,
which always finds a way
to catch your eye,
that rests gently on a fence-line.

The glass from its windows
has found a resting place
in the soil below the sill.

The paint has lost its battle
with the rain and dakota winds.

The roof took a toll
from the harsh winters.

The front door decided
it was time to retire.

The floorboards began to bow
when the rest of its body
slowly gave in to the impending fate.

There is an abode
that rests easy on a fence line
that always catches your eye,
as if hoping for a minute of your time
to tell you stories of its glory days,
just as we do when our hair turns grey.

Carthage, South Dakota

the reality of it all

Countryside homes strew the prairie
like dandelion seeds,
built by calloused hands and cheerful hearts.

Four walls and a roof
full to the brim with joyous memories.

Windows and doors that leak secrets
of struggles during The Great Depression.

There was a day that came
when someone decided
it was time to go.

Was it because one could no longer
come up with the money owed
to keep calling this place *home?*

Sometimes,
my hopeful tendencies break
under the weight of reality
when I realize the tragedy
that can come with abandonment.

However,
these dark memories are meant to decay,
like the walls that bow and the roof that caves
by the hands of constant winds.

The dark memories slowly fade,
but the good ones will always stay,
like the wildflowers that will grow
from the soil that slowly swallows
this countryside home.

Colome, South Dakota

losing purpose

The wind touches the prairie grass
with its wild blades
acting as an ocean,
dancing in unison like waves.

In the middle of this ocean
is a lonely tree
yearning for past times
full of children climbing
its bold branches.

Full of gifts of shade
given by the leaves
to the farmer
after a long, hot day.

Full of perseverance
in the midst of thunderstorms
to prove its dedication and strength.

In this prairie ocean
sits a house in shambles,
next to a lonely tree
that yearns to find purpose,
just as we yearn to find peace,
when our bones grow old.

Colome, South Dakota

where the wind takes us

Seeds of trees find their way
to the soil near houses
left for the birds.

Roots grow deep
into the cellars
that once were filled
with sustenance.

Green leaves turn yellow
and fall towards the earth
as the prairie breeze sweeps
the dancing leaves
through the broken windows.

They find rest on the dusty floors
that once held the tired feet
of the farmer
whose family dwelled
within the walls
that are now weak
and nearing demise.

Seeds of trees find a home
near houses in hopes
to become a part
of their everlasting beauty.

Doland, South Dakota

the myth of certainty

If a house falls after years of enduring thunderstorms
and no one is around to see this final farewell,
do the floorboards still creak one last time?

I think about this
more often than one should.

I feel there is something to be learned here
as I embark on this exploration of the outer world,

for it is just as much
an introspection.

Doesn't our inner world and outer world *collide*
at the crossroads of where we are now
and deeper understanding?

I believe we are meant to
strive for growth
while finding peace
in the uncertainty.

Dallas, South Dakota

a temporary divide

Barbed wire,
unwound in a field,
wraps around and takes hold
of an army of fence posts
methodically placed in a row.

What once was a piece of land
full of oneness,
is split into
a *here* and a *there*.

We tend to enter places
that aren't our own
and call them home,
for a time.

But after many years,
the fence lines weaken
and the houses built
are slowly swallowed by the soil.

And oneness overtakes
the divides we make,
reminding us of the oneness
once again.

Iroquois, South Dakota

the motion of the meadows

I've never swum in the ocean,
but I've waded the fields
to the quietest of places
and found serenity.

The meadows sway to and fro
just as the ocean waves do,
and I submit to the movement
and let it carry me away.

One time,
I was washed ashore
next to an abode
abandoned and left alone.

I traced the spaces on the siding
where paint was missing
with my fingers.

I thought about how
the same motion was used,
many years ago,
to apply the now missing color.

I felt solidarity with
whoever labored to cover
this canvas.

These dakota plains are a museum
full of lost artists waiting for the wind
to form waves
and bring lost wanderers,
such as myself,
near these forgotten pieces of art.

Huron, South Dakota

comfort

There is something about a sunset
that can make the loudest of noises
in one's head fall silent.

There is something about abandonment
that is both chilling and beautiful.

There is something about
the character of the chipped paint
that takes the loneliness away,
as if there is comfort in knowing
someone was before us.

I think this is why
we distress the décor in our homes,
in hopes to feel less alone.

I find peace in the fact
that long after I pass,
one can find comfort in me,
just as the passerby does
in the ruins of
abandoned houses
on the dakota prairie.

Abby Bischoff is a plucky farm kid originally from Huron, SD and spent her summers swimming in stock tanks, taming Hereford cows and naming every barn cat ever. Abby's passion for photography began as a young 4-Her and continued as a journalism major at South Dakota State University. Abby likes indie music and heartfelt television comedies. Her not-so-secret vices are good coffee, baby goat videos, bold lipstick and spending way too much time trying to tame the squirrels in her backyard. She's a proud feminist, advocate and activist for equality and progress. Her Abandoned: South Dakota project has been featured by the Argus Leader, South Dakota Magazine, KELO TV, South Dakota Public Broadcasting and 605 Magazine.

R. H. Swaney is a writer from Sioux Falls, SD who was raised graciously by his grandparents in rural South Dakota. This is where his heart for humanity began to blossom as he navigated racial differences, small-town living, and a complicated family history. His focus is on how his art can affect humanity in a positive, life-giving way. His debut collection of poetry, Lovely Seeds, was self-published in November of 2017 and will be traditionally published, revised and expanded, by Central Avenue Publishing in November of 2018. His work has been featured in publications such as 605 Magazine and South Dakota Poetry Society's Pasque Petals and has been shared by many on social media. When he is not writing, he and his wife Loni Swaney spend their time working on their early 1900s two-story home and going on ice cream dates in downtown Sioux Falls.

CPSIA information can be obtained
at www.ICGtesting.com
Printed in the USA
LVHW07s1226080818
586347LV00001B/1/P